Moving On

GUIDANCE

Janet Lumb
GUIDANCE

Scripture Union
130 City Road, London EC1V 2NJ

© 1985 Janet Lumb

First published 1985

ISBN 0 86201 226 0

All Scripture quotations are taken from the New International Version © 1978 by the New York International Bible Society

Printed and bound in Great Britain at the Bath Press, Avon

Contents

1
Leading questions

Faced with a big decision, most Christians will automatically pray. Shall I be a joiner or an electrician? Should I study English or Economics? Are we to buy a TR7, a Mini or a couple of pairs of roller skates? Should the house be detached, attached or three floors up? Do we go to Majorca this year or Bognor or is it to be a new carpet? Can I know whether to marry Steve or not? We all have our own ideas as to what the major events of our lives are.

What about more common concerns – does the cooker need replacing, shall I buy this pair of shoes, am I justified in buying an ice-cream today? If God cares about the big things, isn't he equally concerned with smaller matters? In fact: 'The very hairs of your head are all numbered' (Matthew 10:30). His knowledge of us is that detailed. Nothing can be dismissed as trivial . . .

Do we have to go looking for guidance? If I don't pray about my new coat, will I get the wrong one – and look like the back end of a camel? How detailed can you go? If I look for guidance for every move, I'll never move!

What does 'right' mean? If it's morally right, is it all right? Or, given two apparently right things, is one more right? Two houses for sale in the same street, at the same price. Is one right for us, and the other one not? How can we know?

If I go wrong, deliberately, is that God's plan mucked up for good? Or do I have to find a long and agonising route back – like the Israelites who married wives who were not God's children – and had to send them back (Ezra 10)! Or what if I take a wrong turning without realising it – does God withdraw from me? Do I have to suffer the consequences for ever? Does one false move ricochet into a whole series of wrong steps, like taking a step on to the wrong down escalator, and having to live with the consequences – or try to run back up, while it moves relentlessly down!

How far wrong will God let us go? As a fairly new Christian with 'L' plates, am I more likely to go wrong? In fact, should I leave the house at all, in case I make a mistake? Do only Superchristians find God's will? How do the greats discover what God wants them to do? How should I in practice go about finding God's will? Are some methods, like putting out sheep's skins to see whether they stay wet or dry (Judges 6:36–40), for the Old Testament only? What is 'just me' and what is God's guidance? Sometimes I just can't make up my mind. What do I do then? In a marriage partnership, is it the man who receives guidance? Are there times when the Lord 'doesn't mind' what course of action we take?

I hope we'll see later, that the things which we see as the most important in life, are not necessarily at the top of God's list; but let's look for a moment at some of the areas of life we consider crucial. How have other Christians found their way to God's will in these matters?

I asked a group of about thirty, aged mainly between

sixteen and twenty-three, when they look to God for guidance. Top of the list was boy-girl relationships and marriage. A job was the second most common, followed by individual needs and problems, in the family for instance, or choice of leisure activity, looking for the right church, finding a house, or choosing school subjects.

Choosing a partner

At a certain Bible college, students had to ask permission before getting engaged. No fewer than seven young men (so the story goes) asked if they could marry one girl. Six of them must presumably have got it wrong! If the girl herself (who must have been quite something!) had been faced with the choice of seven at once, she would have had an extreme problem of guidance.

There are people who think that they made the wrong choice of partner, and that therefore the whole of life is second best. Or they have even opted out of the marriage, on the grounds that it was wrong in the first place. Does God have a Mr or Mrs Right in mind for each Christian? And does he call some to be single and others married, or is it just 'the luck of the draw'? Or is it only the good-looking ones who get married? And if that last question makes us laugh we should remember that some people think that, deep down, and feel hurt as a result.

When it boils down to it, does God know anything about boy-girl relationships these days? Or does he leave it up to us?

Of the married people in the group I asked, none (happily) felt they had married the wrong person – not just because they didn't say so, but because they felt positively that the Lord had guided them to the right one. None of them gave details of how that had happened, but looking back they felt that the choice had been right.

Others had a boyfriend or girlfriend. One at least had faced the decision whether to continue a relationship with a non-Christian. She felt God had guided her to finish that relationship.

Another person, not in that group, was engaged to someone who knew clearly that God wanted him to be a missionary. Because she didn't have the same sense of call, there was some hesitation. After a long and difficult time of waiting, they broke off the engagement. That example shows clearly that God does guide. It would be possible to imagine that those whose guidance was in line with their desires were kidding themselves – not that I think they were! But here God was guiding in a way which was contrary to what the people involved wanted, at least at the time.

You are not likely to find the name of your future wife or husband written in code in Leviticus. What you will find in the Bible, is a framework to work within. There are clear principles, which are not open to discussion. One is the command to marry in the Christian family, not outside of it. It is found in the vivid illustration of a yoke, in 2 Corinthians 6:14, which basically points out the foolishness of 'getting hitched' with someone who is not going in the same direction as you are. The same warning not to marry outside of God's people is repeated many times in the Old Testament. The group were well aware of this principle, and had applied it. They acted on what they knew. The girl who felt it right to finish a relationship with a non-Christian, was doing what she saw as obvious from Scripture though very difficult at the time. They also had the help of being in the fellowship of the church. In other words, they could encourage one another to do right. They could support one another over difficult decisions. They recognised that this was a very important area which could affect their whole future. One suggested: 'It can have a great effect on the whole of our lives, and our spiritual welfare.'

Paul warns that marriage shouldn't be taken on lightly (1 Corinthians 7:33, 34): '. . . . a married man is concerned about the affairs of this world – how he can please his wife – and his interests are divided.' And similarly (verse 34): '. . . . a married woman is concerned about the affairs of this world – how she can please her husband.' He makes it clear he is not saying this to restrict Christians. He does place great weight on a careful decision whether to marry or not, even if you have someone in mind already (1 Corinthians 7:36–38).

Given the principle that he or she, 'must belong to the Lord' (1 Corinthians 7:39) and much advice in the rest of that chapter, in Proverbs 31 (for men!) and other places, there is then some freedom in the decision (1 Corinthians 7:39); this is not a mechanical, but a living guidance. If marriages are 'arranged in heaven', it is with our full participation in the decision, not the kind of arrangement which goes on without our knowledge or consent!

Job

What is God's will for our employment? Are some people called to do a job in order to earn their living and use their spare time for work as part of the church? Is there a special calling only for certain jobs, usually thought of as 'full-time Christian work'? To what extent does God use our natural talents for our work? Is it likely that any of these might be wasted? Does our background set the seal on what we do?

Most of us are influenced in our choice of job by the atmosphere we grow up in. Traditionally, sons took over from their fathers. This is still true in some jobs, particularly, for example, the small business. If there is a lot of talk about cheese in the house, it might influence one of the children to work in a dairy. If there are always bits of electronics around to play with, an interest in that line may well develop (or possibly an aversion!). Clearly, the Lord knows all this, and guides us through our upbringing. He also uses our natural aptitudes – which he has given us in the first place (see Psalm 139).

A mentally handicapped girl could find nothing she was any good at, or was capable of sticking at. The staff in her residential home tried all sorts, until one day she asked to have a go at a lathe. In five minutes she was producing far better work than any of the staff. Her God-given talent was now in use, giving her dignity and a sense of fulfilment. There was no doubt that God had guided her in that direction. It would be ludicrous for her to struggle on with, say, needlework, with no results, when there was something else she had been given the ability to do.

Another person works in a post office job, which has good hours, and no after-hours responsibility. He is very involved in evangelism and youth work with his church. The freedom of his job allows that. Another is a security guard. He does not find his job very rewarding – there are long hours of doing nothing – but he can read then. And he finds great satisfaction in running a small Christian guest house with his wife, which couldn't support them, but which they see as a particular work God has given them. The apostle Paul worked in a similar way. He was a tent maker and would sometimes support himself by making tents while using his free time to spread the good news about Jesus. These two people are working mainly for money (but they make good 'tents'), so that they can do the particular job God has given them, in the rest of their time.

Sometimes it is the other way round. A church might release a teacher from certain duties in the life of the church, so that he can give himself fully to the work at school, with the Christian Union. Christians expect people in some sorts of jobs to have a special sort of 'call'. They usually include ministers, evangelists, missionaries. It's true that people in that sort of job need to be sure God is calling them to that work. But notice in Romans 12:6–8, that the list of gifts which has teachers and prophets in it, also has those who serve and those who give. It is just as important for an administrator, for example, to be sure he is in the right place.

What about being unemployed? Is that a 'calling'? I've met unemployed Christians who felt that it was their own fault. 'Didn't work hard enough at school.' 'Didn't take the job seriously.' These and other statements may be true for some. A lot of other sinners, however, are still in a job! Christians are not immune from earthquakes, illness, death, unemployment . . . Jesus' prayer to his Father for his disciples was, 'not that you take them out of the world but that you protect them from the evil one' (John 17:15). We don't live in a super-cushioned or bionic existence, we take the knocks others do – but we have special protection in difficult situations. God can and does turn a hard situation to our good. I know at least one person who thought that a time of unemployment was God's will for him. Part of the purpose was being able to share his faith with others in the dole queue in a way he couldn't have, if he had been in a job. Another was unemployed for a year or so, and then got a job, working with people who were unemployed. He wouldn't be so effective now, if he didn't know what it is like to experience unemployment. Others have become Christians through being out of a job, and looking for answers to basic questions about life.

Being unemployed can bring real money problems. But

it might be an opportunity which God uses to release someone for other work. 'Work', as the Bible uses the word, is more 'meaningful labour' than 'paid employment'. God doesn't intend us to be out of work in the first sense. God has work for each of us to do. We might not get paid for it though.

Many Christians can point to very clear leading as to which job they should do. The ways they were led are as different as the people.

Take two trained teachers looking for a job. One said to the Lord that she would apply for any suitable job in any area, and trusted him to stop the wrong ones. The other prayed to know where she should apply, and after much thought and prayer was drawn to one particular school, applied for that one job and got it.

Neither seems to me to be wrong, and part of the guidance was no doubt in how they decided to approach the application. The Lord was probably teaching them different things. One felt she had to be willing to go anywhere. That had been a particular problem, as she had desperately wanted one job, and didn't get it. By this discipline, she also applied for a job she desperately didn't want . . . and didn't get that either. (Which shows that God doesn't necessarily want us to do what we don't want to!) The other may have needed to exercise faith, enough to take a risk.

Other big decisions

It might be buying a house. Most people spend more of their money on that than any other single item. So it seems a big decision. Whether to buy or rent, which area, how big, what standard of comfort; on all of these questions the Bible gives principles which help. It helps us to get our priorities right – whether to spend money on that or something else, taking the needs of the poor into consideration, deciding to live in the most comfortable area, or whether God has plans for you elsewhere – all of these are spiritual issues we need guidance on. It might be some other large purchase, a car maybe. Are we more ready to get down on our knees about money than about people? Perhaps not. Some family decisions loom large, like whether to move nearer our elderly relatives, or into an area where our children have more chance of getting a job.

Why do we set so much store by these particular decisions? Because they involve a lot of time, a lot of commitment. They affect other areas of our lives and our development as Christians. They may affect our happiness. And God does guide in these areas. We've looked at a few people who are well aware of that. Who does he guide? His own children. Those who want to be guided by what he wants, who want to obey and be part of his plan. Not only his plan for our own lives, but for the world. When we become Christians, there is a shake-up. How did we make decisions before? On the basis of what we thought best for our happiness, and perhaps for other people we were involved with. Or perhaps on the spur of the moment. There is a whole set of new values involved in being a Christian, not just an overhaul of the old ones. 'If anyone is in Christ, he is a new creation . . .' (2 Corinthians 5:17). We need to take our hands off the things we wanted to take for granted – our standard of living, our ideas about the ideal wife, the work hours we will accept, notions of what we deserve in return for what we do or give. The new values need to come into sharp focus, and we need to be moulded by them in our decisions. If we are firmly fixed in our old standards, we are not really looking to God for guidance. We ourselves have made the rules, and are only asking God to work within the framework we have set. Or worse, we may be just asking him to approve what we have already decided. The new values apply in every area of life. We are not Christian at home, but something quite different at work. We don't have one set of values at church, and one set for our 'private lives'. Being open to God's guidance will involve being completely open. Perhaps letting him point out the areas we tend to close up, possibly without realising it.

There's nothing like a good sea breeze for blowing away the cobwebs. We need to let the Lord do that, by the wind of his Spirit. And the written word of God affects us through its clean air, sometimes biting, always healing. The next few chapters aim to pick up some of the ways Christians look for guidance. Some of them deserve a good laugh. Most of them show how, in spite of us, God does guide his children.

2
The missing piece

Some people think that finding God's guidance in their lives is rather like a game, possibly a jigsaw. The picture is shaping up, but they are looking for a missing piece. Because the piece is actually missing, it will be hard to find. Perseverance, they feel, will be rewarded. So they look for it here and there, sometimes thinking they have found it, then realising that it was the wrong piece after all. You can spot this not-too-rare breed of Christian in one or more of the following ways:

He may be found 'Bible-dipping'. He opens the Bible at random, believing that whatever catches his eye first will be God's word for him. There is a famous story of someone who looked for guidance this way, and his eyes lighted on Matthew 27:5, '. . . he went away and hanged himself'. A little alarmed, but still trusting, he dipped again for confirmation, and the Bible fell open at Luke 10:37: 'Go and do likewise'. To make sure that God was really speaking to him, he tried again, and found John 13:27: 'What you are about to do, do quickly'. What did he do wrong?

1.   He took verses right out of context. He didn't ask 'Why did Judas do that? Am I in the same situation?'

2.   He was only interested in the one missing piece, and not in the whole of God's will for him.

3.   He used the Bible rather like a person might a horoscope — not at all looking for the will of a God who knows everything, but rather playing a game of chance and superstition. He could just as well have used a Winnie the Pooh book, in the same way.

Another similar way of looking for guidance is 'sermon-sifting'. As you listen avidly to sermons, you are looking for one thing only. It is guidance on a particular matter, say whether to move to another district or not. Any hint, sentence, or, best of all, Bible quotation, which might be appropriate to your situation is grabbed and applied. Exodus 33:1 is quoted: 'Leave this place, you and the people you brought up out of Egypt, and go up to the land I promised . . . '. 'Ah, yes', you say 'that's for me!' Christian books can be read in the same way. What's wrong with this approach?

1.   It takes verses or experiences right out of context.

2.   It ignores other teaching, which may be as relevant to you, or more.

3.   It is easy to twist anything to say what you are looking for. It is dishonest.

4.   Again, there is little or no dependence on the Holy Spirit.

Most of us might be blushing slightly here. We must all have taken a similar line sometimes. Certainly particular verses have spoken to us, even at times not strictly in their proper context. The test is whether guidance is based only on this sort of method. If so, it is weak and probably faulty. Often a verse or verses which come up in daily reading, or stand out from a sermon or Christian book, come to confirm

God's leading. That is a very different thing from digging for a verse to back up a hunch or wish. It is God who guides.

Sometimes the person searching for the missing piece might 'lay' so-called 'fleeces'. There seems to be good backing for this from the Old Testament. Gideon did it.

God had promised to save Israel, in battle, from the Midianites, using Gideon as the leader. Gideon was stunned. He was the least significant member of the weakest clan. Gideon asked God to give him a sign 'that it really is you talking to me'. God did that. But Gideon was nervous and unsure. He hit on an idea. He suggested to God that he would put a sheepskin on the threshing floor. If the next day the ground was dry, but the fleece was covered in dew, he would know that God really did intend to use him to save Israel; it was. Then to make doubly sure, he asked God to do the reverse — making the fleece dry but the ground wet — and God did. (See Judges 6 for the whole story.)

We must recognise a lot of ourselves in Gideon's needs. Especially as for him it was a huge task he was about to undertake. He was scared of the Midianites, and afraid of his own people, who had turned their backs on the Lord. He felt totally inadequate for the job . . . He desperately needed reassurance. And God graciously gave it, knowing Gideon's weakness. 'As a father has compassion on his children, so the Lord has compassion on those who fear him; for he knows how we are formed, he remembers that we are dust' (Psalm 103:13,14).

God knows our weaknesses too, and when we are desperate he sometimes gives a special boost of confidence, as he did to Gideon. This doesn't, however, give us the right to ask for such concrete proofs for every small step of guidance we need. 'We live by faith, not by sight' (2 Corinthians 5:7). We have the help of God's Spirit in a fuller way than Gideon. God may not give these concrete proofs. We might have to step out, and only later see confirmation or reassurance that it was the right step. We should beware of claiming sledgehammers to crack nuts (when we should crack them in our own teeth, perhaps!). Such 'fleeces' should in any case be tested in other ways. In Gideon's case guidance had already been given, in a conversation with an angel, and a dramatic sign. Quite proof enough, you might think! The fleece evidence simply backed up what he already really knew to be what he had to do. Gideon was not looking for guidance in some self-centred project. It wasn't a route he would have chosen. Far from it! It would be easy to cheat, where our self-interest is involved. Like the person who wanted to take up a very expensive hobby. He used the lack of enough money as a 'fleece'. When some money came along, he assumed it was for that purpose. Even when the motives are unselfish, there can be a twisting. One person wanted to give Bible study notes to someone she knew. The 'fleece' was that if the girl should meet her, unarranged, that was the proof she needed. However, she hung around near the girl's house, notes already in handbag! She was really pouring water herself on the fleece! Fortunately, God can overrule our daftness, and often does.

Given the rest of biblical teaching, where it seems that the future unfolds step by step (Proverbs 20:24), and in God's time, and in ways he chooses, it would be unwise to make too much of 'fleeces'. There may be times, perhaps when we've a particularly big or difficult decision to make, when a fleece may confirm the way God is leading. We probably already have a good idea of what he wants, and in weakness ask him to show us in a way we find easy to understand. But this should never replace a simple reliance on God to show us what we should do in the way he chooses, and trust in the guidance of the Holy Spirit. Someone who tries one fleece, then another and so on, until he gets the answer he is looking for, is definitely on the wrong track!

The main thing is not that we find a 'missing piece'. It's not as though God finds it very difficult to explain his will. He could speak in any way he chose. He does speak in a variety of ways. But his intention is more than just showing us where to fit in the next step in our lives, and what the next step is. He has more important work to do, changing us to become more like him. We might look at our lives in bits, and see one event, one decision, as more important than another. God has a different perspective. He sees the whole picture, is more concerned with what we are, and wants above all for us to grow up in Christ. All decisions are important, but as part of the whole direction he wants us to take.

I might wonder what job to do. He has that in hand. He knows what it will be, and will show me in his time. But other things are equally important — how do we treat the people around us at a time of tense waiting? What are our motives when we prefer one kind of job to another (is it money, position, power, ease . . . ?) Are we really willing to do anything he wants?

Don't concentrate too much on the decision itself — the job, the car, the stereo, the girlfriend. Do work on your motives. That clears the communication line. (If there's any blockage, it's only at your end!) It can be surprising how simply the rest sometimes follows. God already knows, after all. Generally it is as we get on with daily living that he guides us.

Jesus had strong words for those who fiddled about with details and missed the important things. Matthew 23:23, 'Woe to you, teachers of the law and Pharisees, you hypocrites! You give a tenth of your spices — mint, dill and cummin. But you have neglected the more important matters of the law — justice, mercy and faithfulness. You should have practised the latter, without neglecting the former.'

It isn't that the small things don't matter, but just that if that is all we put our energy into, we miss the sweep of God's purposes, and the 'more important matters' — justice, mercy and faithfulness (see Micah 6:8). An extreme form of this kind of thing is seen in the Neurotic Ditherer. He is conscientious, very. He is convinced of the importance of every action. He wants to find God's will for each move. He will use the three methods above, and maybe others too devious to mention, or multiples of all of them. 'If the next car that comes along is red, I'll cross the road here.' I've seen it in action with someone on a bus with me. I invited her for coffee, but she wasn't sure whether it would be right. She thought she would, then thought that perhaps it wasn't right. As the bus drew up to my stop, she decided perhaps she ought to after all, and got up, to move towards the rear exit. Then at the last moment, as I got off, she changed her mind, turned round and sat down, leaving me just time to step off the bus, and stand on the pavement, wondering where the hidden guidance had come from at that point, and what was wrong with my coffee! God has given us the equipment to make these simple decisions ourselves, so we shouldn't normally bypass this route (our mind). The Lord would make it clear if there was some special reason to do something unexpected. All this person had to decide was (a) whether in friendship she'd like to accept the cup of coffee and chat, and (b) whether some other responsibility was more pressing at that stage.

It has to be said that, though immature, such zeal for God's will is good in itself. Once it learns to relax in his guidance and initiative, and take other people's feelings into account, the desire for the right course of action will be satisfied.

3
Up the garden path

What kind of a God is yours? Where do you get your picture of him? Try piecing together all the impressions of God your mind has recorded. They may have come from all sorts of places – early Sunday School lessons, school RE, your relationship with your father, superstitious sayings you have heard, sentimental pictures. I used to have a childhood mixture of Father Christmas and Father God in my mind. I somehow had the impression that God and the fairies wrapped up the Christmas presents in the clouds, then God (or perhaps Father Christmas) put on his red robes and . . .

So many of the ideas many of us have grown up with about God are faulty. They don't help us understand that he wants the best for us. Is your God a bit of an ogre, maybe even a sadistic trickster?

When it comes to guidance, a lot of us seem to look to a different God from the one we are getting to know. He becomes a teaser, hiding from us the way he wants us to go. We might be lucky and find it, or we might not. There is a 50–50 chance, if that. And it actually seems as though God is trying to thwart our attempts to find his will, just perhaps to see how serious we are. There is no step by step guidance here. It's more a case of keeping your eyes open, and all your wits about you. Then you might chance on the right career, or the right wife, but it's not a foregone conclusion, as there are all sorts of traps and delays on the way.

Not only that, but what he has in store for us is probably the opposite of what we want. Someone may long to be a fireman – that's probably the last thing God has in mind, or so he thinks. Does your mind play that sort of trick? Why do we create that sort of picture of our loving Father? We need to learn that he is all-loving, in spite of the images to the contrary in our minds. God loves to give to his children (eg. Psalm 25:10). He knows what is best for us (Matthew 6:31,32). As we get to know him better, we begin to see and understand what is best for us (Romans 12:1,2). He gave his Son – how can we doubt that he will give the lesser things we need (Romans 8:32)?

Someone who would like to live in the country feels sure that God will ask him to go to the deep inner city. A person who is longing to be married, feels that God will spite him by wanting him to remain single. Another person with a fear of large numbers is terrified God will call him to a public ministry.

There are examples where this sort of thing happens. I know someone who was willing to go anywhere in the world except England (she was not English). She was called to work here. One minister, given half a chance, would run away from the pulpit to a quiet corner. Another person sees the years passing by, and the longed for life partner has not come along. Sometimes there are clear reasons; sometimes we can't see them. Often these callings are what is really 'us' deep down. God knows what our personalities and gifts are best suited to – sometimes those callings are far more appropriate to the real 'us' than we think. There may be obstacles in the way, as in the case of the person who didn't want to come to England. She had to get over a deep-seated resentment against the English. The experience, which she doesn't regret in any way now, has made her a better person.

What we need to learn is to take it on trust when life takes an unexpected and perhaps unwanted turn. If we can't see the reasons, God can. These are some of the reasons why what we expect or hope for is not always the same as the direction the Lord chooses for us:

1. We are shortsighted, and cannot always see now what is best for us in the future.

2. We are impatient, and want a route we can see or move forward on quickly.

3. Our motives are mixed – we may out of self-interest want something which would not be good for us in the long run.

4. We are still learning. The direction God leads us in is often to teach us many things on the way – and not just incidentally. It is his plan to make us like Christ (Romans 8:29).

5. We have too strong a sense of what we could achieve. While we think like that it is not easy for God to use us.

6. We have a wrong sense of priorities. Movement and action and achievement tend to be high on our list. The story of Martha and Mary in Luke 10:38–42 has an interesting lesson. Mary made the better choice in getting to know Jesus better. For all her activity, Martha was not doing God's will.

7. God can see our full potential; we can't. He can do with us more than we could ever imagine. So the reluctant missionary, or minister, or singer, or Sunday School teacher,

or single person, who undertakes these tasks in obedience to God's leading will find that it is in these areas that he or she will be most fulfilled, most at peace.

The grass looks greener on the other side. The young mother with her skirt weighed down by clamouring little hands, sees what appears to her to be freedom and independence in an unmarried friend. Few of us have, like Paul, 'learned to be content' (Philippians 4:12,13) all the time.

There are times of crisis, when it is hard to believe that we are where God has put us. The young doctor working flat out, and called to the ward yet again during the night, feels he has taken on something he can't cope with. A farmer whose stock has been hit by disease, just as he was getting established, feels he must have misunderstood his calling. A teacher is faced with a class she can't stop swinging from the lights. Someone is unemployed, and can't imagine that God has led him to that position. A natural tendency is to make rash judgements within a crisis. It can be very hard to sit tight and ask for God's help, then look back and assess things when the crisis is over. But God may be using a difficulty in our situation for our good. Because we live so much for today, we often find that difficult to understand, and we may doubt God. But looking at these situations from the outside, it's easy to see they can be, not a sign we are on the wrong track, but a chance to trust that the Lord knows more than we do. The crisis is a bend in the river which is still flowing without any doubt towards the sea.

So there are reasons for what seems to be leading us up the garden path. You'll have noticed that all the difficulties in understanding this are of our own making – the Lord of heaven and earth knows what he is doing!

Is there such a thing as chance? I was at a huge Christian gathering the other day, and bumped into the three people I most needed to see. Looking for them would have been impossible in the thousands there. Spending some time in Germany, I met a Christian I knew at a concert – this at a time when I needed fellowship. I met the only other group of Christians I knew in Germany, on a visit to a castle! Christians have lists as long as their arms of such happenings. An onlooker might dub them coincidences – individually. The mass of them for us shows a Father's love and guidance. It is worth noting here, that in the normal run of things, I didn't have a vision or an angel telling me to go to that castle, but since the Lord is in control of all circumstances, it's a small matter for him to allow paths to cross at the appropriate time. For the Christian, nothing is chance, nothing happens without the knowledge and agreement of our Father. This doesn't mean that we are taken out of 'normal' circumstances, incidents, difficulties, or even trage-dies of life. There are times when God does lift us out of what could happen – like the day I inexplicably took a different route to work, and later passed the accident I would surely have been involved in, had I gone the normal way. There are other times when we have to go through the problem, knowing that it is not haphazard or out of control. God himself has allowed it, and is there with us. Every part of life has meaning. The smallest event, the most incidental comment, can turn out to have great significance. Events are part of a chain, one leading to another. We can't tell which are to be the most crucial.

There is one way in which God's plan can seem to go awry. That is our own deliberate disobedience. It is impos-sible to work out what effect that has on our whole lives. If A didn't go to B, where God was calling him, and then married C, whom he wouldn't have met if he had gone to B, and they then have two children, D and E, who wouldn't have existed, if he hadn't met C, and if he had gone to B . . . Some take the view that one act of disobedience means that the whole of life will be second best for A (and probably

C and D and E too). This is to underestimate God's love for repentant A. It also attempts to put God's perfect plan into very human and limited terms. How many of our wrongdoings God forgives, and helps us move on again! We probably don't even notice, half of the time.

We do, however, often have to live with some of the consequences of our sin, particularly where the sin has affected others. Since God knows our failings, and what we shall do before we do it (Psalm 139, Jeremiah 1), he can also take that into account in his master plan. But we'd best leave that to him, and for our part try to put right what we can of what we have done wrong, and look to him for what we do and where we go next. Sin is stepping out of God's plan, because his will for us is to be perfect. The biblical pattern is to repent and start again (1 John 1:9).

For some, it may seem that for a time God is leading in a direction they would not have chosen. For some, sin causes confusion and makes them doubt if they can get back on to the right lines. Very often, however, the Lord leads us in a way in which our (good) inclinations would have taken us.

Think about the place you were brought up in, the people you knew, the variety of experience you had. That is unique to you. God knew that is how it would be for you. These have affected what sort of a person you are now. God's will for you now builds on that. He often uses what you have learned and seen, and how you reacted to it, in the work he has for you and the person he is making you. Did you experience suffering? He will use that (2 Corinthians 1:4). Have there been times when you have known poverty? You may have responded to what you have seen, with a particular concern for the poor. Was your parents' house open to all and sundry? You may more easily be able to do the same with yours. Were you taught to play the piano for years? You will probably make use of that at some time or other.

What about your natural abilities? They are God-given, and you can be sure that you have them for a reason (Psalm 139:15,16). God plans to use them in some way, because you are not just 'thrown together', but 'woven' as you are for a purpose. If you have a creative flair, it may be used in homemaking, or needlework, or joinery, or design, or art, music or drama. It will be used in some way, in keeping with the will of God, who gave it to you in the first place. Are you highly intelligent? There is work for you to do, which will employ that intelligence for the good of others. Have you a good voice? It will be of use, at one level or another. Much of God's guidance follows the lines of what we would have expected anyway. This is because he has not just suddenly started to take an interest in our lives, and is therefore suggesting a few amendments. He has been involved all along, in shaping our personality, in arranging our circumstances. Changes in us are often necessary, to enable our talents and abilities to be used selflessly and not selfishly (1 Peter 4:10,11). Sometimes, too, changes need to take place, so that shyness, reticence, self-despising, false humility, arrogance, or other things which prevent the release and use and development of our gifts can be dealt with. It may be that we have abilities that we have not recognised. These need to be identified, often by others within the church. They then need to be developed by use, as do all abilities.

God also gives gifts for the church, through his Spirit, to individuals. This may mean that someone finds an ability they had not expected, and which may seem surprising, in the light of what they were before. People with very little learning and speaking ability find an understanding of the Bible, and ability to convey that to others. Someone finds an insight into people's problems, being able to discern causes, and give helpful suggestions. Often it is the person whose life has been enriched by such a gift, who is the most surprised by its emerging.

Often the Lord gives us what we want. 'Delight yourself in the Lord, and he will give you the desires of your heart' (Psalm 37:4).

The little boy who fancies being an engine driver may not be in the end. The childish wish may change. The Christian who has hoped, more deeply, for years to become a nurse, may well become one. Sometimes we feel a sort of false disappointment at something not turning out as we had hoped. Or as we thought we hoped. Was that what we really wanted, with all that it would have involved? The answer may be yes, along with other suffering which we do not fully understand. But often we do get what we really want. There may be real hesitation at, say, working abroad. But when it happens, in God's will, the person will find it is really their niche, and they wanted to do it, deep down.

There shouldn't be a sense of guilt at enjoying ourselves! I love my work – that doesn't mean that I'm in the wrong place! There's nowhere I'd rather live – that's more likely to confirm that I'm where God wants me to be, than the opposite. Dare to dream dreams, as a Christian. When they boil down to what you really want, and when they come into line with God's will and mind, you'll find them coming true.

4
Big Bang theory

A group of sixth formers were asked to make a list of ways in which God guides. The list consisted of dreams, visions, prophecies, signs . . . but there was no mention of the Bible, until they were prompted.

'We live by sight, not by faith,' is often our motto. It is the opposite of the Bible's: 'We live by faith, not by sight.' But, in practice, it is a common misunderstanding. We all like reassurance, and perhaps the best reassurance is something we can 'cuddle'. A clear sign, a direct word, a prophecy perhaps, an irrefutable verse, lit up with meaning for the situation in which we need guidance; these are often the things we look for.

Ask experienced Christians how God guided them into a career, marriage or other big decisions. They may well tell you that one or more of these played a part. It is one thing to look back and say, 'That is how God guided me'. It's quite another to say, 'I'm going to ask (and we really mean tell) God to guide me like this'. The way God guides is his choice. He does guide his children if they are obedient, that he has promised (eg. Isaiah 58:9–11). We, however, have no right to tell him how. There may be 'big bangs'—perhaps needed when we are particularly deaf—but if there aren't any, this is no evidence that God isn't guiding. It may be that we have learned to listen and follow him closely enough not to need startling into action.

When there is a 'big bang' it should never be allowed to stand alone. It needs checking by other means. When the church was born, the Holy Spirit spoke to people in visions, sometimes asking them to do quite specific things. In Acts 16:9, Paul had a vision of a Macedonian asking him to 'come over to Macedonia and help' them. Paul didn't dither or hang about. He was ready and off in no time. He believed without question that God was speaking to him. This vision was in keeping with his earlier calling to preach to the Gentiles (Acts 9:15), as well as his natural desire to right the wrong he had done before his conversion, working against Jesus. He did not act in isolation; his companions prepared to go with him, and were therefore presumably in agreement that it was the right thing to do.

God speaks today in visions, and dreams, and many other ways. All should be tested—against scriptural truth. 1 John 4:1 warns us to 'test the spirits, to see whether they are from God.' And the initiative should be left to him. It is easy to use words loosely and claim a 'vision', when what is meant is an idea, a 'picture' when we mean a thought, and so on.

An engaged couple were looking for a house—or rather they were not looking. They had decided that God would show them a house on a particular date. They did find a house on that date, with all sorts of problems, not least that the sellers had to have a house built, before they could move! They wouldn't look at another house in the same area. They got married, and had to live in temporary accommodation, and in the end, the purchase fell through, and they had to start again. In this case, they could have avoided most of their problems, if they had not had a fixation about a particular date, which was obviously, as the conclusion shows, not God-given. If there is to be a 'big bang' in our guidance, we must never initiate it ourselves. All too often, we make the rules, and hope that the Lord will comply. In the following disappointment we may even blame him, or be puzzled that he didn't play our game.

Signs may conflict, be imagined, or twisted. Our active minds are capable of all sorts of self-deception, especially where our feelings are involved. If you are hungry, you will not normally go out into the garden with a large pan and hold it out, in the hopes that the Lord will show you that it's right to eat, by plopping a dressed chicken in your pan, from the sky! You will get food in the normal way. In some special circumstances this sort of thing may happen; for instance, I read today of a group of people in a missionary situation. They were running out of food, and so they prayed. They mentioned in particular fresh fruit, and specifically bananas, at the request of someone in charge of stores. The next day, ten boxes of bananas arrived! The difference is in the situation, and in the need. We should carry on with a 'normal' life—if something abnormal is to happen, because we have an unusual need, we should leave it to the Lord as to how it will be provided. The 'normal' life for a Christian is of course not normal by the standards of other people. It is living by faith that characterises all Christian living, or should do. Why do people want a 'big bang theory' to live from? It must be something to do with a desire, seen not only in Christian circles, for excitement, or even thrills. There is a thirst for adventure, but preferably the spectator kind.

Whilst the Lord can and does speak at times through

the earthquake, and the wind, and the fire, he may be more often heard in the 'gentle whisper' (see 1 Kings 19:11–13).

5
If it feels good...

'How can it be wrong, when it feels so right?'
'I felt I should train to be a teacher.'

Feelings and feelings. The trouble is, with something which involves me so personally, I can go to extremes. I can either make all judgements by my feelings, trusting them rather than my mind or common sense, or what anyone tells me . . . or I can suppress all feelings, and wait for hard facts, before I will move an inch.

Much of the problem is in what we are using the word to mean. We might define feelings as the desires, the emotions. And there are related words we could use to expand the definition: longing, passion, excitement, compassion, enthusiasm, lust. All of these are part of our make-up: all (except lust!) have their place. It would, however, be foolish to act on them alone.

Why aren't these feelings reliable? Proverbs 14:12 says, 'There is a way that seems right to a man, but in the end it leads to death.' Things aren't always what they seem. There are circumstances which influence how we feel about something.

If a friend is very enthusiastic about an idea, we might easily catch it.

If someone is tired, they are more easily influenced by some kinds of feeling.

The time of day, or of the month, or of the year, might affect how we feel about things.

A lot of us live in great dependence on feelings: they determine what we do, whether we get up, how we treat people, whether we carry out an act of kindness, whether we follow something through to the end, or give up half-way.

Feelings (on this definition) can be used for good, on the other hand. If you are feeling enthusiastic about the job God has given you to do, you will probably get twice as much work done. If you feel compassion when you see someone hurt or suffering in some way, you are more likely to reach out to them in their need. 1 John 3:17,18 is about having compassion and acting on it, by caring about someone we see in material need, and helping him or her. There is also quite a different kind of 'feeling'. This could lie behind the second sentence at the beginning of this chapter. 'I felt I should train to be a teacher', may not refer to a one-off and passing feeling. It is probably not something she felt when she got up in the morning, rather like indigestion, and which she then took to mean something. It is probably a conclusion which has been arrived at after much thought and prayer, with advice from others, a growing idea which may have been with her for a year or two, or more. This person is using the word 'feeling' quite differently. It's important to make a clear distinction.

We have already mentioned the Bible college, where

those who wanted to get engaged first had to ask the Principal's permission. Many an earnest student had to nervously inform the Principal that he had found the one he was looking for. But of the seven men who went to tell the Principal they felt it right to marry—and to marry the same girl—clearly at least six of them were wrong! There are several issues there, but one of them is that they had simply followed their feelings, and then called it guidance. The outcome shows that they were misguided.

'How can it be wrong, when it feels so right?' . . . *when the Bible says so*. For example, it is never right to commit adultery. Exodus 20:14 stands, however right a wrong relationship may feel in a particular situation. In this area of sexual feeling, it is particularly easy to be misled, because the emotion is so powerful. We must beware of mistaking 'I want it' for 'It is right'. Very strong feelings are often saying the former. To twist what they are saying, is to deny what God has already said, and he doesn't change his mind on such matters.

'How can it be wrong, when it feels so right?' . . . *when time, or experience, prove it to be wrong*. The person who felt it was right to become a doctor, pursued that 'calling' against all the odds. She didn't achieve the necessary exam grades. She kept trying until she got on to a medical course. She frequently failed exams. She failed in the end. Clearly it was not right for her to become a doctor.

'How can it be wrong, when it feels so right?' . . . *when it denies a biblical principle*. There is not a verse for every situation (how mechanical life would be, if there were), but there are principles, which help us to work out our actions at a deeper level. People like Wilberforce, who worked against the slave trade, were not motivated by a verse, but by great and lasting principles—of equality in God's sight, of love for the poor, of compassion. All from the Bible.

Slavery might have felt right to the masters, to the privileged. But biblical principles tell us otherwise.

How can you tell which kind of feeling you have? Every Christian must have had trouble with this. I feel it's right; how do I know whether I am misled? How do I decide whether it is only my emotions speaking?

There are some concrete ways of finding out. If biblical facts or principles are being denied, it's the feelings which are wrong. If the outcome is different, the feelings were misguided. I have on occasion felt very strongly I should buy a particular house. When someone else got there first, or made a higher offer, I knew my feelings had been wrong.

Feelings should be tested. That includes sounding out the opinion of others, checking out the biblical principles and anything specific the Bible may have to say on the subject, praying and often waiting. Let the feelings be exposed to as much experience as possible. For example, John feels he should leave Manchester and go to work in Sheffield. It's unlikely that he feels that without any lead-up or warning, or without there being any other factors, such as his job coming to an end. If, however, it does happen to be a sudden feeling, he would then need to look at the job situation in Sheffield, for work similar to what he is doing now (if he has a job). He would need to see whether there was a church where he could become an active member. He'd need to ask Christian friends what they thought of the move. He'd need to examine his motives. By this time, the idea would either have disappeared, under the weight of difficulties, or have become a distinct possibility. In other words, he is moving forward, but carefully, 'knocking on doors', as Christian jargon has it.

How can you know if your 'feeling' is only misguided emotion? If we change the word for the second kind of feeling we have discussed, to 'discern', it helps to clarify the issues. 'I feel I should buy a new car' could simply be subjective, only my emotions. 'I discern I should move to Manchester' carries more weight. It shows that there has been thought, that the decision has not been taken lightly, that the mind as well as the emotions is involved. It is this kind of discernment Christians need to develop. It is learning to hear the Master's voice. 'My sheep know my voice . . .' (see John 10:4). It is learning to distinguish that voice from other voices (John 10:5). It is learning to be willing to hear God's voice. By God's voice we mean what he is directing us to do, by whatever means. It is developing a closer relationship with him, so that I begin to know what he thinks (Romans 12:2). It is being single-minded enough to hear the voice and act on it, before other voices crowd in. From the *outside* it is difficult to see whether someone else is being guided by God or their emotions. But from the inside, for myself, it is hearing and knowing and understanding what God is saying to me, in whatever way he chooses.

The emotions are part of our God-given equipment for making decisions, but only part. Most of us would be unhappy with a marriage match which was made from a list of qualities and qualifications. Running down the list, a man might be heard to mutter, 'Excellent cook, enjoys sport and music, sense of humour and very reliable. Right, I'll take her.' Such a response is barely human, (though it might work!) and denies a whole part of his make-up. On the other hand most of us would be unhappy if a chance meeting under the autumn leaves with a background of golden sunset, turned into an immediate proposal of marriage, with no other knowledge of each other.

This might seem to labour the point, but how many of us make other important decisions in a surge of emotion, be it missionary zeal, or tired impatience? The worst thing is an attempt to spiritualise the feeling, and label it as though we had felt (discerned) something, when really we had only felt (felt) it.

A friend of mine, a recognised lover of food, would often say, 'I feel led to have a cream cake.' He never intended the statement to be taken seriously. In fact, more recently, he has—more convincingly—felt led to have fewer cream cakes! In short, it's not good to say, 'I feel I should . . .' or 'I feel led to . . .' when you mean, 'I feel I'd like to . . .'. We should learn to discern God's will, 'by the renewing of your mind' (Romans 12:2). The verse goes on: 'Then you will be able to test and approve what God's will is.' Those who live and act on feelings alone, will soon get into a tangle, or conflict of choice.

There are times when someone acts, apparently on impulse. They have 'felt it right' to do something, and they have gone and done it. There was no build-up, and no warning, and no time-lag to test it. It may be that God has spoken to them very clearly and directly, and more of that in the next chapter. But the proof is in the outcome. That will show to the onlooker whether it was an impulse, or a directive from God. There are times when a person does something that 'breaks all the rules' of guidance. Gladys Aylward did, when she went off to China on her own initiative, against all advice, and with no support from a missionary society. If she had been a friend of mine, I would probably have advised her not to go. I would have been cynical when she went. I would have been nonplussed when God used her with such power, vindicating her decision and making it clear she was right. An onlooker could only think she was acting on emotional impulse, and misguided at that—until the proof came in the outcome—the evidence of the rest of her life. It can only be said that this was an exception. Gladys was well able to discern and sense God's will, to the extent that she knew it was right to go. The Lord will make it very clear if you are to do something so out-of-the-ordinary by such an unusual route. In that, he won't ever go against his own principles, only perhaps against our idea of how he normally works.

To know how it can be wrong, when it feels so right, I need to know more than feelings alone. In particular, I need to know more clearly what God has said for all time in the Bible.

Paul tried to enter Bithynia (Acts 16:7), but the Spirit of Jesus would not allow him to. It doesn't say how Paul knew, but it was likely that he felt strongly that it was not what the Spirit of Jesus wanted. Similarly the Spirit 'compelled' him to go to Jerusalem (Acts 20:22). Some Christians say they 'felt constrained' to do something—quite a quaint expression which perhaps, if used honestly, means they were 'compelled' by the Spirit, like Paul.

In 2 Corinthians 2:13, God guided Paul by unsettling him. Because he 'had no peace of mind' he moved on. This was for a very human reason, to look for Titus, whom he had expected to see in Troas, but who wasn't there. Someone who is close to God can feel in that way disturbed and ill-at-ease where they are, if it is God's time for them to move on. They are sensitive to his will, and in that way 'feel it right' to go. Just to throw a spanner in the works, it is also possible for Satan to prevent us doing something. In 1 Thessalonians 2:17,18, Paul says he had 'intense longing' to see the Thessalonians, but Satan stopped him, despite repeated efforts. Isn't life going to get complicated here? How do I know whether something is hard to achieve because the Holy Spirit is stopping me, or the devil? The answer is in knowing and distinguishing the voices. The reassurance is that Jesus said of the shepherd, himself: 'His sheep . . . know his voice. But they will never follow a stranger; in fact, they will run away from him because they do not recognise a stranger's voice' (John 10:4,5).

In case it seems to be getting difficult, here is how Paul sums up the problem of sorting out our mere emotion, which may be wrong, from the leading of the Spirit: 'So I say, live by the Spirit, and you will not gratify the desires of the sinful nature. For the sinful nature desires what is contrary to the Spirit, and the Spirit what is contrary to the sinful nature' (Galatians 5:16,17). It is the whole of our lives that is important, not just isolated moments. If we are consciously allowing God's Spirit to control us we shall find that we fall into line with his plan for us.

6
Private line

Sometimes new, or not so new, Christians are impressed to hear another Christian say: 'The Lord told me to . . .' They wonder whether all Christians should be able to hear the Lord so clearly. They wonder what the person really means, what the voice sounded like, how they knew it was the Lord speaking . . .

In some circles you can hear lots of Christians talking like that frequently, and may feel quite inferior if your 'private line' to God doesn't seem to be working as well as that!

When someone says, 'The Lord told me to . . .', it is possible that:

a. He did!
b. They want to convince you, and you can't argue with 'God'.
c. Their feelings are active.
d. Lots of other people talk like that, and they don't want to seem less spiritual.

43

e. They think that is what the Lord wants them to do, and want to make it sound more definite than that.

How do you know which it is? If you read any biographies of godly Christians, times when they claim God speaks to them verbally are very few, if ever, in a lifetime. Yet people do hear the voice of God in words, on occasion, perhaps at a time of crisis or crucial decision.

When Saul was on a journey to Damascus, he heard the voice of Jesus: 'Saul, Saul, why do you persecute me?' (Acts 9:4). Others heard the sound of the voice, too, so it was not just in his head. This became the moment of Saul's conversion, a dramatic moment, both for him, and the whole Christian church.

Later in the same chapter (verses 15,16), the Lord spoke to Ananias in words, reassuring him that Saul, who had persecuted the church, was now a believer, and was chosen to bring the good news to the Gentiles, to those who were not among the historical people of God, the Jews. These were words of great significance, which were then able to be written down to help us too.

At other times, as we saw earlier, someone may know very clearly what the Lord wants them to do, by a variety of means. They may then use the expression, 'The Lord told me to . . .', but this can be rather misleading. It's a claim that should be confirmed by their quality of life as a Christian. This makes it seem more likely that a person could have this kind of understanding of God. Other tests should also be applied, similar to those we apply to feelings: Is it in harmony with the Bible's teaching and principles? Does the 'pudding' turn out right with these ingredients?

There are, of course, huge dangers in saying, 'The Lord told me to . . .' if it is not true. It's a phrase which doesn't allow for much discussion or contradiction, and it may be presumptuous. It doesn't make room for others to make their suggestions. If it becomes acceptable to talk like that casually, it becomes easy to fix it to anything you want to do. (Compare, 'I feel it right to . . .'.)

What if God doesn't speak to me like that? Am I doing something wrong? In reality the experience may not be as common as casual expressions would have us believe. In some ways this is perhaps sad; it seems that at the times of great power of the Holy Spirit being unleashed, 'the word of the Lord' is often heard. There were lean times in Israel's history. In the days of Samuel, for instance, there was such a time: 'In those days the word of the Lord was rare' (1 Samuel 3:1).

As we have seen, we should learn to hear and discern what God is saying. It's not that he doesn't speak clearly enough, but rather that we don't or won't or can't hear. Other 'voices' may attract our attention, other interests obscure our interest in what he wants to say in our lives. We may have to sort out our motives, as to whether we want to hear and do what he says. This comes from a growing communication. As with any relationship, as we get to know God better we understand more clearly what he says to us: by reading the Bible, where he has spoken clearly to all Christians, in prayer and thinking about him, in living our normal lives in obedience to him and seeing how he deals with us and works in our lives. I have occasionally met Christians whose prayer and time alone with the Lord starts at 5 a.m. or thereabouts. They seem peculiarly in touch with the will of God. There's no short cut to putting ourselves in tune with him and his voice.

Sometimes a 'private line' consists of prophecy. An individual receives a message he or she feels is from God, and for a particular group of people, or perhaps one person. The person who has received the message passes it on to the person or people for whom it is relevant. It will often relate biblical truth to a particular situation; it never goes against Scripture and does not have the same authority as Scripture. Much of preaching is prophecy; prophecy is the 'cutting edge' of preaching. When the preacher is relating a biblical truth to everyday living, and the people present think, 'Crumbs, that's meant for us!' or 'He must know all about me', it is likely to be prophecy at work. The apostles in the New Testament had a particular ministry, which carried special authority. The teaching which they gave as they were guided and instructed by the Holy Spirit is unique; it forms the basic foundation of Christian truth. Even they sometimes got it wrong (see Galatians 2:11), although the writings they have left us are completely trustworthy. Other prophets did not have the same level of authority. Those who heard had to 'weigh carefully what is said' (1 Corinthians 14:29). Prophecy is given an important place in the life of the church. It is the spriritual gift Christians are to desire especially (1 Corinthians 14:1). It builds up the church by, 'strengthening, encouragement and comfort' (1 Corinthians 14:3), and is therefore more important than the gift of tongues, which only edifies the individual concerned. Everything good which God gives can be twisted. The main danger with prophecy comes when we do not allow it to be tested. If it starts with phrases like, 'The Lord is telling you to . . .' or 'Thus says the Lord . . .', this implies that if we test it, we are testing the Lord.

Someone told a fifteen-year-old girl that the Lord was calling her to be a missionary in Nigeria. Fortunately the church leaders were wise, and advised her to wait and see how things developed, to see whether it was true. If they had not advised her, she could have suffered unbearable pressure. She didn't want to be a missionary, and if it was not right, could have spent an anxious several years, waiting for the unhappy event. God equips those he calls, not those he doesn't. If there is no corresponding inner call for the person concerned, confirmed on the way by events and developments, the prophecy can be taken to be false or to have been misinterpreted or wrongly applied.

We must test prophecy (1 John 4:1). There are false prophets, who prophesy in the name of Jesus (Matthew 7:22,23). The church must discern. So it is a contradiction to start a prophecy with a phrase like, 'Thus says the Lord.' A prophecy must be open to be tested, and an introductory phrase like, 'I think the Lord is saying to you . . .' is a much humbler approach, and one which allows the prophecy to be weighed by the church leaders and others. Whatever language is used, and however vivid the imagery, the prophecy should be tested. As a rightly used part of church life, prophecy will help the church to grow into Christ, being applied to the body in just the places it needs it, and stimulating healthy growth. In the Bible, prophecies related to everyday life and its realities, like possessions, ambitions, sexual purity, feeding the hungry.

Paul said, 'Do not put out the Spirit's fire; do not treat prophecies with contempt. Test everything. Hold on to the good. Avoid every kind of evil' (1 Thessalonians 5:19–22). That sums it up.

No 'private line' should be 'ex-directory'. When God really speaks directly to and through an individual, it is powerful and for the good of the whole church. No one has a private claim to communication with God which they may protect from the comments, encouragement and evaluation of others.

7

In it together

The principle with which we concluded the previous chapter can be taken further. In fact, no one has a private claim to protect any part of their Christian lives from scrutiny of the right sort. Just as he or she was born in a natural way into a family, so a Christian is born a second time, into a church family. This is both a help and a responsibility, and a check against peculiarities.

We British like to keep ourselves to ourselves. 'Everyone is entitled to his own opinion.' 'Let sleeping dogs lie.' 'An Englishman's home is his castle.'

These are common attitudes. Some areas of life are commonly considered sacred. People may become offended if others make suggestions as to how they should bring up their children, where they should live, what kind of car or cooker they should buy. But the church is meant to be much more involved with each other than that. We are called to biblical community, not Western individualism (see Acts 2:44-46).

In some churches, this is only true of certain matters, considered 'church business'. That is only the beginning. It is however very encouraging where there is unity in the body over things like evangelism, improvements to the church, the minister's salary. I was at a church members' meeting, where there were two strong opinions as to where the minister's house should be. In the course of discussion, one opinion gradually melted away, and it emerged that the other was the one to go for. As a body we had, I believe, found the mind of Christ on the subject. There had been long discussions, but there was no sense of triumph by those of the one opinion, or defeat for the others. As we had come together to find out what God wanted, he had honoured that. It was as the church at Antioch was together that the Holy Spirit guided them to set apart Barnabas and Saul for missionary work. The whole church then took the initiative, and 'sent them off' (Acts 13:3). The same church later sent Barnabas and Paul to deal with a church problem which had arisen in Jerusalem. The Jerusalem church similarly chose Judas and Silas to go back to Antioch with Paul and Barnabas. Not so much of the lonely, 'Lord, where do you want me to go?'; more the community of the church sending people off for the good of the church and its work, with full support and knowledge and encouragement.

These incidents and other examples are reported as though they were normal. If today's church took on the same responsibility more often, perhaps there would be some pews noticeably vacated!

Most of the New Testament letters are sent, not to individuals, but to whole churches. They were not for one person to deal with, but for the building up of the whole. This is not spelt out. It is just assumed to be normal. We in the Western world are in the position where we have to fight against our inbuilt reserve, and reluctance to 'interfere' with others' lives, or let them 'tamper' with ours. New

Testament believers did not have that to contend with, for their society was more interdependent, though they still needed to learn how that was to work out in the church. The 'body language' of Ephesians 4 emphasises how the members of the church are Christ's body together. Any resources the individuals have are for the body and its development (Ephesians 4:11–13). It follows naturally that the Holy Spirit would guide the church, the body. The question is, 'What is God's will for the church?', and individuals are chosen to be a part of that. In Acts 15 the church at Jerusalem, inspired by the Holy Spirit (Acts 15:28,29), sent a letter to the Gentile believers about the problem which had come up about circumcision, and Judas and Silas were to confirm it by word of mouth. They may have been thinking, 'What does the Lord want me to do over the next few months?', but the main thrust of what they are about to do is for the good of the church, and is decided by the church.

There is an important safeguard here. Where an individual cooks up a plan, it may be:

a. merely for self-fulfilment
b. a madcap idea
c. unrealistic
d. inappropriate to his or her gifts
e. impossible
f. in need of support

just to mention a few possible difficulties. Where other Christians are part of the decision, there is strength in it. Ecclesiastes 4:12 says, 'Though one may be overpowered, two can defend themselves. A cord of three strands is not quickly broken.' Jesus makes it clear that when Christians gather he is with them, 'Where two or three come together in my name, there am I with them' (Matthew 18:20).

The other extreme is where the individual has no say in

the matter; and we have already looked at that briefly. The individual should weigh up advice he receives, in the light of the Bible, and in private prayer. We are all responsible for our actions. God does not give anyone absolute right over the decisions or lives of others. We must take very seriously the advice of other Christians especially leaders, particularly when they have spent time in praying about God's way for us, but blind obedience is never required of God's people. He looks for *responsible* obedience.

It might have been inconvenient for Judas and Silas to go off at that point. They might have had new wives, or new babies, or been in the middle of some important work. What is clear though, is that the work of the gospel came first. They must have been able and suited to doing the job, and so were sent. No doubt the community which sent them out would also take care of any responsibilities they were leaving behind. Such is the strength of the community of the church. On the surface of it, life seemed to work out so simply in those days, and be so straightforward. We on the other hand might be aware of long and painful waiting, while our church gets organised to help us make vital decisions. We might feel they misunderstand what we are asking, we might be sorry the church did not take more initiative, we might be hurt by advice thrown at us with a lack of prayer and thought. Nevertheless, the advantages outweigh the disadvantages. By involving the rest of the body in our major decision-making, we may be helping the body to function properly, as well as taking another step towards discovering the direction the Holy Spirit is leading us in.

8

The mind of Christ

The word 'guidance' does not appear at all in the New Testament of the New International Version, and only seven times in the Old. It is clear, though, that God does guide his people. Why doesn't the Bible give me detailed advice about how to decide which job, boyfriend or stereo is right?

We are consumers; we think in terms of commodities—goods we can buy, things we can have. So places, things, times become very important for us. The Lord has different priorities; he is not preoccupied with these things, nor does he intend us to be. Jesus made this clear: ' . . . seek first his kingdom and his righteousness, and all these things (food, clothes, tomorrow's needs) will be given to you as well' (Matthew 6:33).

It's a worthwhile test to ask ourselves whether we put as much effort into working towards the establishment of his kingdom and the development of our individual and communal righteousness, as we do wondering about where we should live, what we should buy, who we should marry

. . . (There are connections, but it is a question of which matters take up the bulk of our time and energy.)

One of the things Timothy is strongly encouraged to do by Paul, is to: 'Flee the evil desires of youth, and pursue righteousness, faith, love and peace, along with those who call on the Lord out of a pure heart' (2 Timothy 2:22). The idea of pursuing righteousness must be completely new to a new Christian. He has probably been pursuing all sorts of things—happiness, the good of his family, wealth, success, acceptance with people, a comfortable home . . . Now he is to put the same sort of energy into pursuing righteousness. This will mean time spent studying the Bible, to find out what God means by righteousness. It will involve time spent in prayer, to apply what it means to his own life. It will mean enthusiasm expended on good things, the good of others; it will involve action, of the sort he has probably not bothered with before. A Christian accountant left a job in which he was expected to fiddle the books. He put righteousness first. A new job came up very quickly. He had not put the job security first, but willingness to do what was right resulted for him in a job being 'given to (him) as well' (see Matthew 6:33). We shouldn't, perhaps, give the impression that a job will always turn up so quickly in similar circumstances, but the Lord will always honour those who put his kingdom first, in one way or another.

The Lord does not promise to guide his children, with no strings attached. Conditions are spelt out clearly to God's children, the Israelites, in the Old Testament:

'If you do away with the yoke of oppression, with the pointing finger and malicious talk, and if you spend yourselves on behalf of the hungry and satisfy the needs of the oppressed, then your light will rise in the darkness, and your night will become like the noonday. The Lord

will guide you always; he will satisfy your needs . . . '
(Isaiah 58:9–11)

It is no wonder it is sometimes difficult to hear what God is saying! It's like being on an Inter City 125, and hanging out of the window eagerly at every station to see whether it is Birmingham. All your luggage is ready for you to leap out; your ticket is handy to show at the gate; you have every expectation that Birmingham will show up on the station sign in a while. What you haven't realised is that you're on the wrong line! All the eagerness and preparation were a waste of time; you boarded the train from York to King's Cross, so you weren't even going in the right direction!

If I have £5,000 in the bank (we can all dream!), I may spend a long time thinking and praying about whether I should buy a new car, or a small extension to the house. But if I don't even consider whether the money should be diverted 'on behalf of the hungry' or some other need, I may be on the wrong line altogether. I am not really open to God's guidance. I am only expecting him to bless one or other of the courses of action I am suggesting to him. To 'spend yourselves' on behalf of those in need is basic. It is God's character, which he wants us to share. As we start to want what the Lord wants, we begin to find out more of what that really is. Many of our pet ideas will have to go, much of our thinking will be shaken up and remoulded. Instead of putting up our own suggestions all the time, as to how God could best work, we start to wait for his initiative, to let him direct us in whatever way he chooses, not just within the limits we set him. To depend on God rather than 'myself' is one of the important lessons a Christian has to learn (and re-learn, and learn again . . .). Paul considered the hardships he and others suffered in Asia were for the express purpose, 'that we might not rely on ourselves, but on God' (2 Corinthians 1:9). James puts it very clearly:

'Now listen, you who say, "Today or tomorrow we will go to this or that city, spend a year there, carry on business and make money." Why, you do not even know what will happen tomorrow. What is your life? You are a mist that appears for a little while and then vanishes. Instead, you ought to say, "If it is the Lord's will, we will live and do this or that." ' (James 4:13–15)

James is not recommending a formula. He is talking about a way of thinking, an attitude which is to become deeply ingrained for a Christian. So the reflex action is not, 'what shall I do?' but, 'Lord, what shall I do?' It is the dependence of a child with its arms stretched out, expecting help from its father. For the child it is a natural gesture.

In this picture, although the child reaches out for the father, he expects his father to stoop down and take him in his arms. The initiative, strength and significant movement will come from the father. Speaking through Joel the prophet in the Old Testament, the Lord promises:

' . . . I will pour out my Spirit on all people.
Your sons and daughters will prophesy,
your old men will dream dreams,
your young men will see visions.' (Joel 2:28)

God will take the initiative. He is able to show his people what he wants them to do. We don't need to get into a tangle, as though the Lord might not be sure what he wants, or needs our help to sort it out. Our dependence on God, and expectation that he will take the initiative, leads to a lack of anxiety about material things, and small things, and details. The Lord's Prayer was Jesus' model prayer for his followers. It concentrates on general things, not specific details. It stresses the need for God's will to be done, and only then mentions material needs in broad outline. They are summed up as 'daily bread' (Matthew 6:9–13).

It was not a request for fish and chips, a new bike and a three bedroomed semi. Jesus assumed that his Father knew of the particular needs. He makes that clear a little later (verse 32). Are some of our prayers for guidance petty? It is possible sometimes that we can't see the wood for the trees. We are so busy focusing on details of what God might want us to do, that we can't see the sweep of God's plan. We fail to see the general direction he is urging us in, the lessons he is teaching us.

I have found it wonderful to discover that God does look after the details, in providing material needs. He even, it seems, has an interest in colour schemes, details of time planning, the people I'll bump into and when. But not because I get churned up about these things. Rather because he is the God who created the beauty of colour. He is the God of order and not chaos. He has a deep interest in where his creatures go, the relationships they make. In fact, 'all these things will be given to you as well.'

We need to be much more aware of the 'Godness' of God. He is not a man. We shouldn't mentally limit his character to that of a man. He can cope with all our needs. But his plan goes beyond our immediate needs.

'For my thoughts are not your thoughts . . .
As the heavens are higher than the earth,
so are my ways higher than your ways
and my thoughts than your thoughts' (Isaiah 55:8,9).

'No-one knows the thoughts of God except the Spirit of God. We have not received the spirit of the world but the Spirit who is from God' (1 Corinthians 2:11,12). It is the Spirit who will help us tune in to God's thoughts. Tuning in is a sensitive business. On the radio, a slight twist of the hand and you have passed the station you were looking for. But when you are on exactly the right wavelength you know, because the sound is clear and true. God's Spirit 'searches all things, even the deep things of God' (1 Corinthians 2:10). He is finely 'tuned in' to God the Father. He interprets to us the thoughts of God. He draws our attention to them in the Bible, he reminds us at opportune moments of the things we know and have experienced of God. This is true to the extent that, 'The spiritual man makes judgements about all things' (1 Corinthians 2:15).

At the heart of the spiritual person is obedience. Peter and John were in a difficult position. They were told by the High Priest not to speak any more in the name of Jesus (Acts 4:17). But Peter and John not only knew what God wanted them to do, they were prepared to do it, in spite of the opposition. 'Judge for yourselves whether it is right in God's sight to obey you rather than God' (verse 19).

John spells it out clearly: 'This is love for God: to obey his commands' (1 John 5:3). So our closeness to God will grow as we obey him. Often, if we are honest, it's not so much finding God's will as doing it which is difficult. Do we have a tendency to go on looking for guidance when it is quite obvious what we should be doing? This is particularly true in many moral issues. The Bible is clear what should be done. Greed, jealousy, sexual immorality and other twistings of God's purposes are always wrong. It's no good asking for guidance, when one course of action we have in mind would take us along one of those roads. We already have our guidance. God won't change his mind on the moral absolutes. 2 Corinthians 6: 14–16, for instance, makes it clear that any 'yoke' or close bond with those who are not Christians is not allowed. It is no good to keep asking, hoping that he will stretch the rules. He has spoken.

When Jesus uses the illustration of the sheep and the goats for the day of judgement (Matthew 25:32–46), the 'goats' were full of excuses about their behaviour. They had not cared for the hungry, thirsty, stranger, naked, sick, imprisoned. I suppose they had hoped that the King would not notice; they could get away with that, as long as they appeared pious in his presence. What they did not realise was that Jesus the King took their wrongdoing as a personal insult. It was as though they had refused to care for him in his need. It is no good giving excuses, when we know very well what we should do. No further guidance is necessary (though we are often exercised as to *how* to care for those in need). There is never any need to ask, 'Should I care for this needy person in front of me or not?'

There is a principle in God's scheme of things, that if someone is faithful over a few things, he will be put in charge of many things. Any developing Christian will see the truth of this, as he 'tries his wings' on small responsibilities, then discovers he is trusted with greater ones (see Matthew 25:14–30). This is often how God guides, gently as we obey and honour him in the smallest tasks.

'Whatever you do, work at it with all your heart, as working for the Lord, not for men' (Colossians 3:23). Paul is speaking to slaves in particular here, but this is relevant to any situation, perhaps especially when our tasks seem to be the humble and unnoticed ones. How do we respond now to caring for that one person in need? What kind of an inward expression do I have, when I'm asked to do the least exciting job in the church? How seriously do I take my responsibility for the small and unreliable Sunday School class? I am amazed at how seemingly insignificant tasks and incidents in the past, have been preparation for work later. It's a mistake to value some tasks and despise others. 'Whatever you do' includes the least popular and most hidden jobs. If no one cleans the bathroom, the house is in chaos in the end! This is true literally and figuratively!

As I respond to the tasks the Lord has put in front of me I develop, and receive more responsibility. My character grows as it is exercised. Someone might be very patient. His patience develops as he is put in a situation which tries his patience. Someone else may relate well to older people—he is able to do that better as he relates to them and understands their needs.

A specific call to particular work is usually clarified and tested in this way. The Lord may have taken the initiative in giving you a deep concern for a particular country, or section of society, or age-group. In your normal Bible reading, passages seem to stress this. Comments from others, and advice from experienced Christians add weight. As you take seriously the responsibilities you have at the moment, the call takes shape and develops; it becomes more specific.

You want God to guide you. Study thoroughly the ways he works in the Bible. Learn about his character. Dig out the principles for living. You won't, for example, find a verse about whether you should buy the Rolls or not. You will find vital principles relating to: obsession with material things (Matthew 6:19–24), the pros and cons of wealth (Matthew 19:21–26), giving to the poor (2 Corinthians 8:14,15), giving to help missionary work (2 Corinthians 8:1–12). These principles will go part or most of the way towards helping you make the decision.

Don't think that you come with an open mind. You already have attitudes, some subconscious. Some of those commonly held on the subject of wealth are:

'Luxury is O.K. as long as it's not too obvious.'

'As long as I don't seem richer than the other members of my church.'

'It's for the sake of the children.'

'I've worked hard for this, I deserve it.'

'God has prospered us, we accept it gratefully.'

They need to be put under scrutiny, under the magnifying glass of Scripture, so that the flaws show up.

There are principles for every decision. Some decisions are more complex than others. They are usually complicated because you or others have made them so. But because they are complicated, that does not mean there is not an answer.

It is not that we turn up the 'rule book' every time we want to make a move, or decision. The descriptions of the Bible as a rule book or manual rather like a car manual are true up to a point, but not completely accurate. It is the living word, and its truths, which are God's truths, are to become part of our lives.

Jesus was able to answer the devil on every point, as he tempted him. The devil was even able to quote Scripture (Matthew 4:6), but only by twisting the principles. Jesus knew the principles, of course. They were as natural to him as breathing, because he understood the character and ways of his Father. And in perfect obedience, he applied them to every situation.

God does have a plan. It is his plan. He has masterminded it. It is perfect. It is prepared in advance (Ephesians 2:10). We Christians are a part of it. The main thrust of God's plan for Christians is the 'good works' he has for us to do. He wants us to become like Jesus, who 'went around doing good' (Acts 10:38).

Paul's prayer to God for the Ephesians was for them to 'know him better'. All the decisions and happenings of our lives work towards that purpose (Romans 8:28,29). This should be the goal of your life. If you aim for that then: 'all these things will be given to you as well. Therefore, do not worry about tomorrow . . . ' (Matthew 6:33,34), because 'your heavenly Father knows that you need them' (Matthew 6:32). With the single exception of the period before the

Holy Spirit came at Pentecost, you don't read of New Testament Christians sitting about doing nothing until God shows them where to go, or what to do. You find them in prayer about big decisions. You find them getting on with what God has given them to do for now, and in the process, he leads them on to somewhere else. The Lord is concerned with the whole of our lives. He does guide his children. We can be right in the heart of his will. He cares about who we are and who we become, as much as where we are. His will is best.

God is love, and he helps us in our weak faith. We should look for growing understanding of his mind. We should not rely too heavily on 'props' and 'visual aids'. When you are learning to ride a bike, there comes a time when you have to take the stabilisers off, having learned how to balance. Feelings, too, should be used, not abused. He has promised wisdom to those who ask for it (James 1:5), because, 'we have the mind of Christ' (1 Corinthians 2:16).

If you have found this book helpful you will want to read the rest of the Moving On series

The Bible

    John Eddison

The Church

    Nigel Wright

The Holy Spirit

    Clive Calver

Jesus

    Frank Cooke

Prayer

    Jim Graham

Saving Faith

    Roger Forster

Man and the World

    David Jackman

Lifestyle

    Roger Sainsbury

Temptation

    Jill and Bob Moffett

Sharing Good News

    Phil South

God

    Steve Brady